DISCOVERING GEOLOGY

FOSSIL FOCUS

CORALS

An Earthwise™ publication

Corals (or more formally, Zoantharia) have mobile larvae that become sessile (fixed to one place) after a few days. They are marine animals related to jelly fish and sea anemones, but lacking a free-swimming (medusoid) stage. They may have first evolved during the Precambrian and are still found living today. Some, like octocorals (the polyp has eight arms), are soft bodied and rarely preserved as fossils, but others secrete a hard calcarous skeleton and are thus important rock-forming organisms. We focus here on the three groups (or orders) of corals that are most frequently found as fossils — **Rugosa**, **Tabulata** and **Scleractinia**.

Corals: the animal

Corals comprise a soft bodied animal **(polyp)** that lives in a calcareous skeleton **(corallum)**. Food is taken in and waste products are discharged through the **mouth**, which is surrounded by **tentacles** with poisonous **stings**.

The polyp removes calcium carbonate from the sea water to create a skeleton of calcite or aragonite, although, when fossilised, aragonite often changes to calcite. The cup (or **corallite**) in which the polyp lives is strengthened by **septa** (radiating plates), **tabulae** (corallite floors which build up one on the other) and sometimes **dissepiments** (small concentrically arranged plates between the septa). Corals may live alone (solitary) or in a group (colonial or compound).

Soames/Summerhays/Biofotos

Living coral — open polyps of *Tubastrea*.

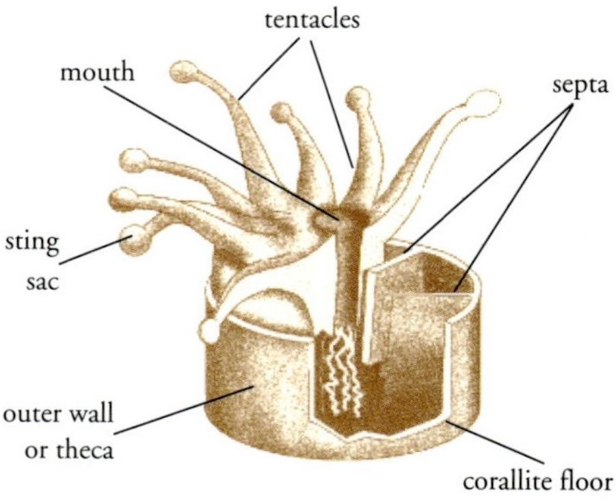

An imaginary solitary coral, partly broken away ▶ to show the calcareous structure of the corallite.

Rugose corals are solitary or colonial types with bilateral symmetry. They have a hollow in the top surface (a **calice**) in which the polyp sat, together with numerous tabulae, septa (the major ones being arranged in groups of four), dissepiments, and some have a central calcareous rod (**columella**).

Lithostrotion basaltiformis a colonial rugose coral from the Carboniferous of Derbyshire. Lateral view *(above)* and cross-section *(below)*.

Dibunophyllum bipartitum from the Carboniferous of North Wales, a solitary rugose coral. Side view *(left)* and cross-section showing septa and dissepiments *(right)*.

Tabulate corals are all colonial and have many closely spaced tabulae, but septa and dissepiments are either absent or very weak. Their fossils are often preserved as a cluster of long, slender tubes (corallites).

Palaeofavosites rugosus a tabulate coral from the Silurian of May Hill, Gloucestershire, England.

Corals through time

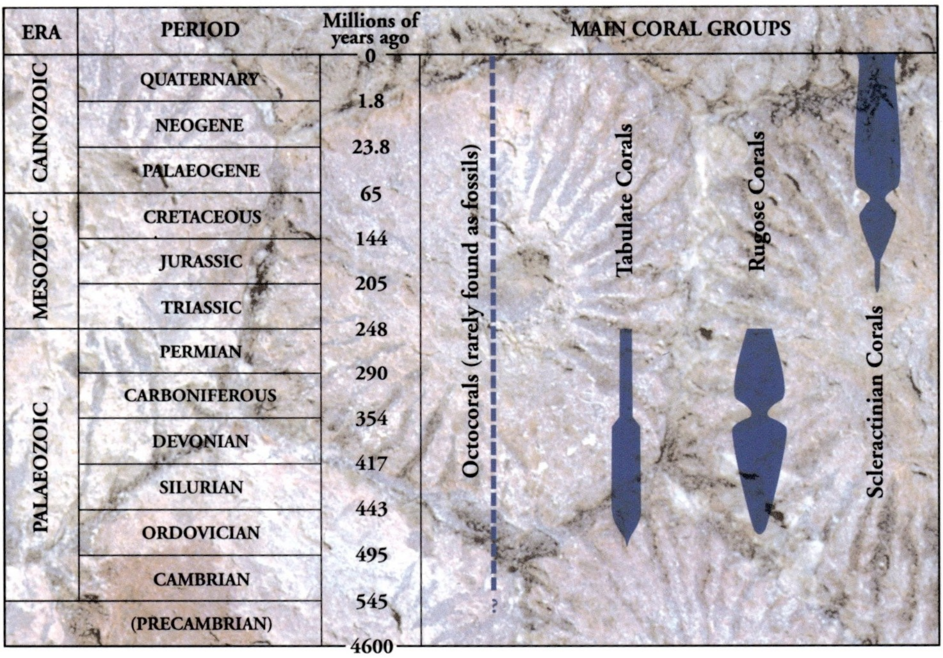

Background image: *Cyathophyllum tinocystis* from the mid Devonian of Ogwell, Devon.

The distribution of corals through time

Corals may have evolved first during the late Precambrian, if *Charnia* is correctly identified as an octocoral, but rugose and tabulate corals became common only in the Palaeozoic *(above)*. A period of mass extinction took place at the end of the Permian, when over 90% of all invertebrates became extinct, including all tabulate and rugose corals. The reason seems to have been due to the formation of the super-continent Pangaea and the disappearance of environmental niches. This was also a time of increased aridity, changes in ocean currents, more competition for less space on the continental shelf, widespread occurrence of evaporite deposits, intense volcanicity and changes in sea level. Scleractinian corals, which evolved during the Mesozoic, replaced the extinct groups.

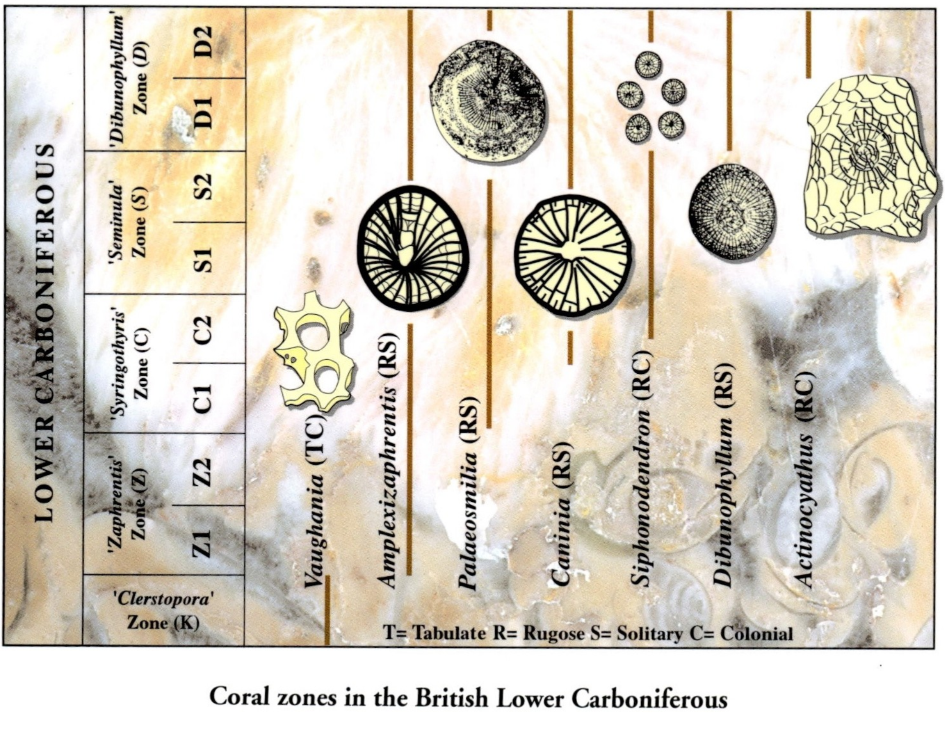

Background image: *Lithostrotion araneum* from the Carboniferous of Avon, SW England.

Coral zones in the British Lower Carboniferous

One of the most important uses of fossils is in biostratigraphy, where short-lived fossil species are used to date the rocks in which they are found. Coral species are usually too long-lived to be useful in this way, but Lower Carboniferous rocks of Britain can be subdivided into zones defined by the first appearance of key corals they contain *(above)*. These zones can also be traced throughout western Europe.

Editor: Martin Litherland; Design: Jennifer Evans; Photography: Paul Tod & Tim Cullen; Illustrations: Chris Wardle

Coral reefs

Tabulate and rugose corals built mounds and thickets contributing to reef building during the Palaeozoic and commonly seen in Silurian to Carboniferous rocks of Britain. On a world wide scale, they seem to have lived in equatorial latitudes in a similar distribution to modern forms. Since the Triassic, scleractinian corals have become reef builders. Coral reefs range in size from a few metres to hundreds of kilometres, but they fall into three main types: fringing reef, barrier reef or atoll.

A **fringing reef** forms when coral reefs grow in warm, shallow coastal waters. Sudden changes of sea level, such as during the last Ice Age, kill the coral, but where sea level rises (or the land sinks) at a slow rate, coral growth can keep pace. ▶

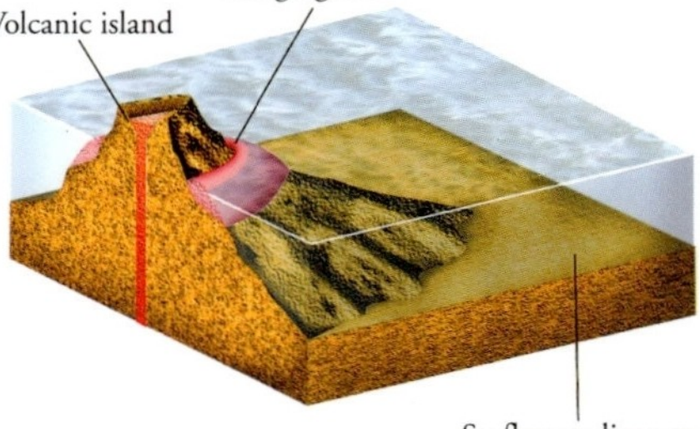

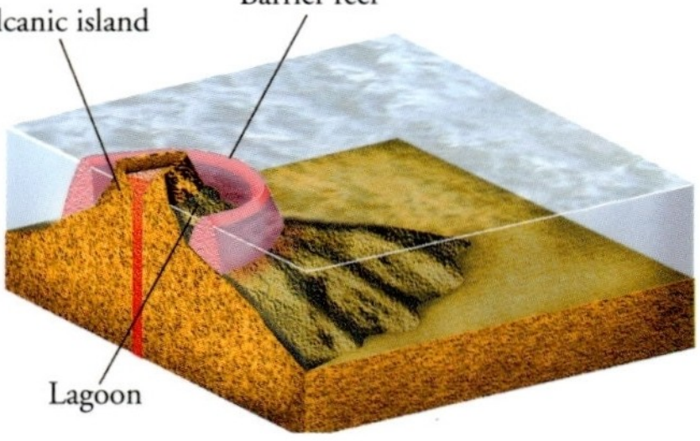

◀ The volcanic island has subsided slowly and the reef has grown upwards at the same rate. In this way the reef has formed a **barrier reef** a little way from the shore and with a lagoon behind it.

Continued subsidence (or rise in sea level) causes the volcanic island to disappear below the waves. The reef, however, continues to grow, taking on a roughly circular shape (an **atoll**) and enclosing a lagoon, floored by sediment and reef debris. ▶

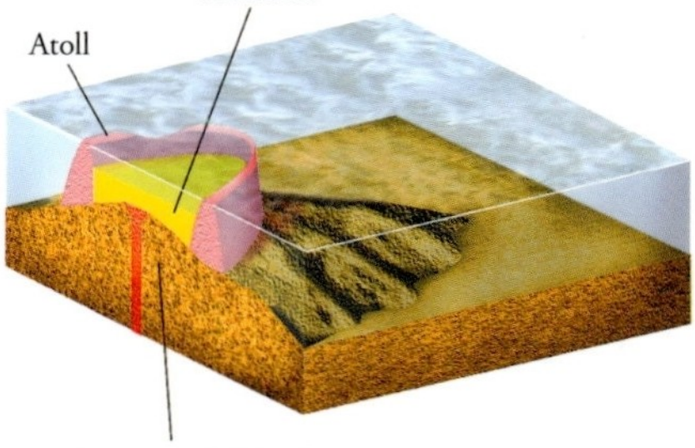

(× ½)

Halysites catenularia a tabulate coral which contributed to reef building in Britain during the mid-Silurian. This specimen is from Dudley, English Midlands.

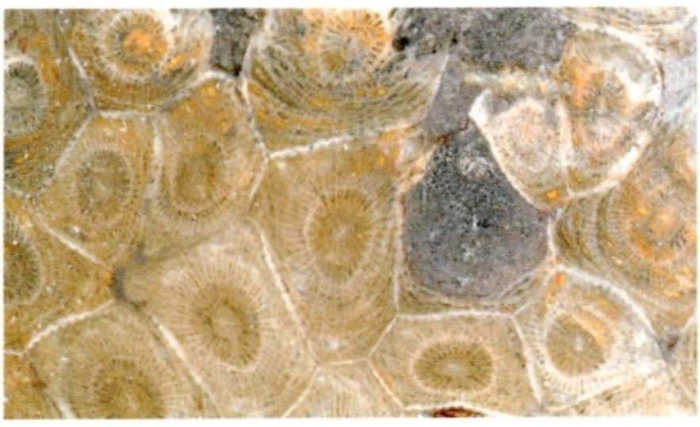

Actinocyathus floriformis, a colonial, rugose coral that contributed to reef building in the tropical waters of south-western England early in the Carboniferous. (× 1)

(× ¾)

Siphonodendron junceum, a colonial, rugose coral from the Carboniferous of Ecclefechan, southern Scotland. The cross-section *(left)* shows the septa, dissepiments and columella. The side view *(right)* shows the columella and many tabulae, one on top of the other.

FOSSIL FOCUS — CORALS

Scleractinian corals may be solitary or colonial. They have a very porous or spongy skeleton made of aragonite and strengthened by radiating septa (the main ones being arranged in groups of six), dissepiments and sometimes a columella. They may have evolved from a soft bodied ancestor.

Isastrea conybeari, a colonial scleractinian coral from the mid-Jurassic.

(× ½)

Flabellum woodi, a solitary scleractinian coral from the Pliocene (late Neogene) of eastern England.

(× 1)

(× 1)

Acropora, a modern scleractinian coral from the latest Quaternary of the Pacific showing the spongy aragonite skeleton.

Heather Angel

A living coral reef in the Seychelles where Stag's horn *Acropora* coral and yellow soft coral give shelter to many organisms including the fish *Abudefduf*.

Corals: their environment

Corals live in marine water, at most depths and latitudes. They have been found in water 6000 metres deep, but are most common at depths of less than 500 metres. At these depths, the water temperature may be close to 0°C, but corals are most common between 5° and 10°C. Deeper water corals are mainly solitary, although some, such as *Lophelia,* are colonial and form thickets and banks.

Close-up of a modern colonial coral *Lophelia pertusa*, dredged up from the Stanton Banks off Scotland.

Corals reefs on the other hand, are restricted to the warmer regions of the world's oceans such as the Seychelle islands in the Indian Ocean (*above*). They gradually add skeletal calcium carbonate to the existing reefs to build huge structures in well lit, warm, tropical waters, clear of land-derived sediment. Reef-building corals favour water depths of less than 10–20 metres and temperatures between 25° and 29°C.

(× ⅓)

Fungia, a modern solitary coral from Indonesia.

Corals: fact or fiction?

The coral clock

When corals are examined under a microscope, their outer surface can be seen to be made up of hundreds of ridges (about 200 per centimetre). Each ridge was formed in a single day as the coral grew. Modern corals, such as *Manicina* and *Lophelia* have about 360 growth ridges per year on average (it varies a little as they do not grow during breeding or bad environmental conditions), but Devonian corals like *Heliophyllum* and *Eridophyllum* grew 400 ridges each year on average. This is because the Earth's rotation has slowed down so that there are 35–40 fewer days in the year now compared to Devonian times.

Heliophyllum halli lived during mid Devonian times in Michigan, USA. Annual and monthly growth rings can be recognised *(top)* and when magnified, daily growth rings can also be seen *(bottom)*. Growth rings show there were about 400 days in the year during the Devonian period.

Tisbury Starstone: in Wiltshire, Upper Jurassic Portlandian rocks yield the colonial, scleractinian coral *Pseudodiplocaenia oblonga* in which the numerous radiating septa form a stellate pattern *(see inset)*.

Starstones

In his book The Natural History of Oxfordshire (1677) Robert Plot wrote about star stones, including '... *Astroites, which in the whole are irregular, but adorned as it were with a Constellation*'. *Astroites* is in reality a Jurassic coral and probably *Pseudodiplocaenia* or *Isastrea*. Robert Plot did not know what they were, but wondered if they were *'formed of some latent plastick power of the Earth'* or *'some way related to the Celestial Bodies'*.

The earliest corals

Octocorals are rarely found as fossils as they lack a hard skeleton, but many palaeontologists believe that one of Britain's oldest known animals, *Charnia*, belongs to this group. Faint impressions of this soft-bodied animal have been found in late Precambian rocks of central England and southern Wales and very similar fossils have also been found in Australia.

A plaster cast of *Charnia masoni*, a 600 million year old, soft bodied sea pen, considered by some to be an octocoral, from the late Precambrian of Leicestershire. On death it toppled over onto soft volcanic mud on the sea bed leaving a weak 'finger print' before it rotted away entirely.

Fossil Focus: Corals by Ian Wilkinson & Colin Scrutton.
Earthwise is a trademark of the British Geological Survey, Keyworth, Nottingham NG12 5GG

ISBN 0-85272-349-0

9 780852 723494

British Geological Survey

£1.95

For information about other BGS publications, please contact the Sales Desk at the address above (Telephone 0115 936 3241; Fax 0115 936 3488; E-mail: sales@bgs.ac.uk).

Cover photo: *Thamnopora cervicornus* a mid Devonian coral from Torquay. (Actual size) ▶